Cites &
Sources

An APA Documentation Guide

Cites & Sources

An APA Documentation Guide
Revised Third Edition

Jane Haig
Georgian College

Vicki MacMillan
Georgian College

Gail Raikes
Georgian College

NELSON / EDUCATION

NELSON / EDUCATION

Cites & Sources: An APA Documentation Guide, Revised Third Edition

by Jane Haig, Vicki MacMillan, and Gail Raikes

Associate Vice President, Editorial Director:
Evelyn Veitch

Editor-in-Chief, Higher Education:
Anne Williams

Executive Editor:
Laura Macleod

Marketing Manager:
Amanda Henry

Developmental Editor:
Theresa Fitzgerald

Permissions Coordinators:
Jane Haig, Vicki MacMillan, and Gail Raikes

Content Production Manager:
Susan Wong

Proofreader:
Wendy Thomas

Indexer:
Gillian Watts

Production Coordinator:
Ferial Suleman

Design Director:
Ken Phipps

Managing Designer:
Katherine Strain

Interior Design:
Heather Holm

Cover Design:
Heather Holm

Cover Images:
Top left to right: © Heather Holm, © Johanna Liburd, © Heather Holm; Bottom left to right: © JUPITERIMAGES/GOODSHOT/ Alamy, © Heather Holm, © Heather Holm

Printer:
Transcontinental

Library and Archives Canada Cataloguing in Publication Data

Haig, Jane
    Cites & sources : an APA documentation guide / Jane Haig, Vicki MacMillan, Gail Raikes.

Includes bibliographical references.
ISBN 978-0-17-647350-1
[Rev. Third Edition
ISBN 978-0-17-650406-9]

1. Bibliographical citations–Handbooks, manuals, etc. 2. Report writing–Handbooks, manuals, etc. I. MacMillan, Vicki II. Raikes, Gail III. Title. IV. Title: Cites and sources.

PN171.F56H36 2010
808'.027   C2008-906966-8

ISBN-13: 978-0-17-650406-9
ISBN-10: 0-17-650406-0

Table of Contents

Acknowledgements

We acknowledge and appreciate the suggestions and comments of colleagues, students, and friends for this third edition of *Cites & Sources*. It was prepared in response to recent changes in APA formatting for electronic sources and requests for further information on plagiarism. To that end, we have included new electronic research formats and examples, updated print and non-print in-text citations and reference page examples, and expanded the section on avoiding plagiarism. The majority of examples have Canadian content.

We acknowledge with gratitude the contribution of Colleen O'Brien, a graduate of Laurentian University, for permission to use her essay, "We'll Rant and We'll Roar Like True Newfoundlanders: Newfoundland Nationalism."

In particular, we thank Heather Holm, our designer and photographer for the text. We appreciate her insightful guidance on incorporating design features that make the text current and accessible for students and a viable "teaching tool" for the classroom. The photographs with their accompanying quotations add visual interest and are in keeping with a "green" theme for this text. We believe that raising awareness of the fragility of our planet is everyone's responsibility and this is one small measure on our part to do so.

Introduction to APA

The American Psychological Association (APA) style of documentation is commonly recognized as a standard documentation style for colleges, universities, and businesses.

A consistent style of documentation in research papers

- Provides uniformity to the paper
- Allows readers to give full attention to content
- Presents ideas in a form and style accepted by and familiar to readers

This revised third edition is updated to reflect changes, particularly in referencing electronic sources, in the sixth edition (2010) of the *Publication Manual of the American Psychological Association*. Changes are noted with a star.

NEW

"We are so small, and the great aerial ocean so vast, that it seems hardly credible that we could do anything to affect its equilibrium. Indeed, for most of the past century humans have held to the belief that climate is largely stable, and that the flea on the elephant's buttock that is humanity can have no effect. Yet if we were to imagine Earth as an onion, our atmosphere would be no thicker than its outermost parchment skin."

Tim Flannery, 2005

1 Getting Started

Selecting a Research Topic

Once you have selected a topic for research, you need to consult many sources, including books, magazines, newspapers, and online information.

PLAGIARISM

To avoid plagiarism, you must document all ideas and direct quotations in your paper using APA style. (See **Plagiarism, p. 5)**

Proper documentation requires that you

1 Acknowledge source references within your paper (See **Section 4: Citing Sources**)

2 List your sources at the end of your paper (See **Section 6: Reference List Entries**)

Documentation in the Essay

NEWFOUNDLAND NATIONALISM   5

While the media might have weakened Newfoundlanders and their identity in the early 20th century, it has done much for the cultural nationalism that is prevalent today. As Millard, Riegel and Wright (2002) argue, "The relative decline of state institutions as transmitters of cultures and identity in favour of commodified expressions of these goods may be affecting the tone and content of Canadian Nationalism" (p. 2). So, too, does the commodified expression of Newfoundland's pop culture transmit her identity to the rest of Canada and the world.

Reference List Entry

NEWFOUNDLAND NATIONALISM   9
References

Millard, G., Riegel, S., & Wright, J. (2002). Here's where we get Canadian: English-Canadian nationalism and pop culture. *The American Review of Canadian Studies, 32*(1), 11-34.

Overton, J. (1988). Newfoundland culture? *Journal of Canadian Studies, 23*(1), 2-22.

Story, G. M., Kirwin, W. J., & Widdowson, J. D. (Eds.). (1999). *Dictionary of Newfoundland English* (2nd ed.). Retrieved from http://www. heritage.nf.ca/dictionary

Research

Your research begins with evaluating print and electronic resources to determine the most useful sources of information for your report or paper.

Consider the following criteria:

ACCURACY

Is the information contained in the document both **relevant** and **accurate**?

Check the publisher/producer for **credibility**.

For example:
A government publication such as *Statistics Canada* can be considered **reliable**.

A Web site developed by someone interested in promoting a particular point of view or product using **questionable** statistics may not be reliable.

CONTENT

Is there enough **detailed** information on the topic?

Is the information at an **appropriate level** for the topic?

CURRENCY

Is the information **up-to-date** and/or **relevant**?

If the information is from a Web site, when was it last **updated**?

AUTHORITY

Who is **responsible** for the information?

Is the producer/publisher the same as the author?

Are **credentials** listed?

Is there an advertiser/sponsor relationship?

Is the resource wiki-based, allowing anyone to contribute?

Note: While Wikipedia may be a good place to start your research, it is generally **NOT acceptable as an academic reference** due to its questionable reliability.

OBJECTIVITY

Is the information **biased**?

Is the producer actually an advertiser **promoting** a product?

If the resource is a Web site, check the domain name for clues to ownership.

Taking Notes

Research involves taking notes in which you summarize, paraphrase, and directly quote information from your reference sources.

Be sure to include all of the information necessary to correctly document your sources when it comes time to write your paper.

While taking notes, clearly distinguish between paraphrased material and direct quotations, and always include the following:

NOTES

1 Title of Material Used

2 Author's Name

3 Pages Consulted

4 Publication Data: Date, Place, and Publisher

5 Access Information for Electronic Materials

Unbelievable as it is, some student papers contain, in varying amounts, quoted or paraphrased text from a source **without any in-text citations**.

APA requires **BOTH** an **in-text citation** and a **Reference list entry** for each research source used in your report or paper.

You can't have one without the other!

Plagiarism

Plagiarism is the presentation of someone else's words or ideas as your own – and is a **serious academic offence**. Whether you are quoting or putting an idea or fact into your own words, you must cite your source (see *Section 3: Citing Sources*).

PLAGIARISM

Plagiarism will not be an issue or a temptation if you have a **detailed plan** in place to write your paper and you ensure your own ideas form the basis for your thesis (central argument).

For your planning, take into account the following:

1 complexity of the topic
2 research required for the topic
3 time available to complete the paper

PENALTIES

Penalties for plagiarism, even if unintentional, may range from a **zero** on the paper to **expulsion** from the institution. Protect yourself by scrupulously documenting all your sources.

AVOIDING PLAGIARISM

You can avoid plagiarism and its subsequent penalties by following these guidelines for your paper:

1 **Keep records** of all the sources you consult during your research and note-taking. (See *Taking Notes* on the previous page.)

2 Use your research notes to support, not replace, your own ideas.

3 Prepare a draft of the Reference list as you work.

4 Check to ensure all your **sources are documented** before submitting your paper.

5 Never copy and paste from electronic sources without documentation.

6 Never submit a paper purchased or copied electronically from a writing service.

7 Never submit a copy of someone else's paper as your own.

Examples of Plagiarized and Correctly Documented Text

Here are examples of plagiarized and correctly documented text using the same source text.

The original text was taken from the March, 2008 article, "Fat of the Land," in *The Walrus* magazine. The article is a research source in a student paper on healthy eating.

ORIGINAL TEXT

"On December 12, 2005, Canada became the first country to require food processors to label for the presence of trans fats in their products. Twenty days later, the US Food and Drug Administration followed suit. Trans fats, found in vegetable shortening, margarine, crackers, candies, cookies, fried foods, baked goods, and other processed foods made with partially hydrogenated vegetable oils, raise low-density lipoprotein (LDL or 'bad') cholesterol, increasing the risk of coronary heart disease" (Payton, 2008, p. 46).

Payton, B. (2008, March) Fat of the land. *The Walrus*, 5, 46–53.

EXAMPLE (PLAGIARIZED TEXT IN BLUE)

PLAGIARIZED: Slight Changes in Wording (Words Left Out)

Researchers realized the harm that trans fats were causing and urged the government to take action. Canada became the first country to require food processors to label for trans fats in their products. The US Food and Drug Administration followed suit. Trans fats, found in processed foods made with partially hydrogenated vegetable oils, raise low-density lipoprotein cholesterol, increasing the risk of heart disease. Consumers benefited from this action as manufacturers, forced to source out reliable alternate fat sources, …

CORRECTLY DOCUMENTED: Direct Quotation

Researchers realized the harm that trans fats were causing and urged the government to take action. A recent article in *The Walrus* commented that foods such as "margarine, crackers, candies, cookies, fried foods, baked goods" laden with trans fats have major health implications and can raise "the risk of coronary heart disease" (Payton, 2008, p. 46). With this legislation, consumers now can make more informed choices when purchasing processed foods.

CORRECTLY DOCUMENTED: Direct Quotation

Researchers realized the harm that trans fats were causing and urged the government to take action. In his article on palm oil, an alternative to oils laden with trans fats, Brian Payton (2008) noted that trans fats "raise low-density lipoprotein (LDL or 'bad') cholesterol, increasing the risk of coronary heart disease" (p. 46). With legislation and public awareness, food processors were forced to source out alternate sources of fats such as palm oil that would offer similar texture and taste in foods.

CORRECTLY DOCUMENTED: Paraphrased

Researchers realized the harm that trans fats were causing and urged the government to take action. According to an article in the March, 2008 issue of *The Walrus*, legislation requiring food processors to acknowledge the amount of trans fats in their labelling was passed in late 2005 in Canada and early 2006 in the United States (Payton, p. 46).

CORRECTLY DOCUMENTED: Paraphrased

Researchers realized the harm that trans fats were causing and urged the government to take action. According to Brian Payton (2008) research concludes the use of trans fats in processed foods leads to increased bad cholesterol and the ensuing risk of heart problems (p. 46).

Photo © Heather Holm

"I was surprised at the number and variety of brilliantly-coloured butterflies; they were all of small size, and started forth at every step I took, from the low bushes which bordered the road."

Henry Walter Bates, 1873

Formatting Your Paper

Formatting Your Paper

A successful research essay or report must be professionally formatted and presented. First impressions count!

This section presents a **sample title page, essay and report models, and reference page formatted** according to the following APA guidelines. Consult with your instructor or refer to other documentation manuals for more detailed information on formatting and organizing specific kinds of reports.

MATERIALS AND TYPEFACE

Use good-quality 8 1/2" x 11" white paper. Select **Times New Roman, 12 point**, as the preferred font. All documents should be word-processed and printed using a high-quality printer.

TITLE/COVER PAGE

Begin your paper with a **cover page**. Place a **running head** in full caps one inch from the top and flush with the left margin. On the same line, indented five spaces from the right margin, place the **page number**. Centre and double-space the text in the upper half of the page. Use **mixed case letters** to type the following: the **title** of your paper, your name, the name and **section** of your course, your **instructor's name**, and the **date**.

PAGE NUMBERS AND RUNNING HEADS

In full caps, type a **running head**, an abbreviation of the title, flush with the left margin of every page including the title page. The running head has a maximum of 50 characters, including letters, spaces, and punctuation. Beginning with the title page, **number all pages** including the cover page, tables, appendices, and the references page.

MARGINS, SPACING, AND INDENTATION

Use **one-inch margins** (2.54 cm) on all sides of the page (top, bottom, right, and left). **Double-space** the entire paper, and **indent the first line** of each paragraph one tab. **Tab indent** each line of long quotations (longer than forty words), and double-space the lines of the quotation.

HEADINGS

Headings help to organize the presentation of your research and are required for most reports. Because it is assumed that your first paragraph is the introduction, do not use "Introduction" as a heading. Centre and bold **first-level headings** (major divisions) and use mixed case letters. Left justify and bold **second-level headings** and use mixed case. Bold and indent **third-level headings** one tab from the left margin. Capitalize the first word only, place a period at the end of the heading, and begin the paragraph immediately following. For documents requiring more than three levels of headings, refer to the APA manual.

ABSTRACT/SUMMARY

An abstract or summary provides an **overview** of your paper. It should include your **central idea**, **key points**, and any **implications** or **applications** discussed in your paper. Consult your instructor for more specific details and requirements.

An abstract or summary **immediately follows** the title page. Type "Abstract" or "Summary" as the main heading, **centred** and at the top of the page. An abstract or summary does not usually exceed one page.

APPENDIX

An appendix is located at the **end** of a report following the **Reference list** and contains additional information referred to in the report.

For example:
You might want to include a **copy of a survey** form (questionnaire or interview questions) that you used to collect data for your report. Each appendix is labelled **Appendix A, B, C**, and so on, according to the order it is referred to in the report.

SUPPLEMENTARY MATERIAL

Specific kinds of reports may require **additional** supplementary materials – such as an **executive summary**, a **memo** or **letter of transmittal**, **interview transcripts**, and so on.

Ask your instructor or consult your course textbook for how to arrange and place these supplementary materials.

VISUALS

Reports often include visuals to clarify and summarize research findings. Visuals are used to **complement** rather than to duplicate text.

Tables, for example, present exact numerical data arranged in columns and rows.

Figures include graphs, charts, maps, illustrations, drawings, and photographs.

Tables and figures allow readers to see the overall **pattern of results**, eliminating the need for lengthy discussion.

DO NOT include any visuals that you do not clearly introduce and explain in your text.

Ask your instructor for specific assignment guidelines on placing, labelling, and numbering the pages of your visuals.

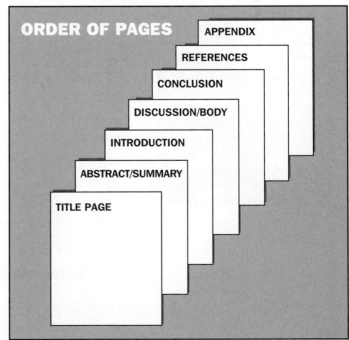

ORDER OF PAGES

- APPENDIX
- REFERENCES
- CONCLUSION
- DISCUSSION/BODY
- INTRODUCTION
- ABSTRACT/SUMMARY
- TITLE PAGE

Sample Cover Page

Centre information in upper half of page and **double-space**

A Indent **page number** five spaces from right margin; on same line, include **running head**, flush left, and in full caps

B **Title** in **mixed case**

C Student's name

D Course name

E Instructor's name

F Date

A NEWFOUNDLAND NATIONALISM   1

B We'll Rant and We'll Roar Like True Newfoundlanders:

Newfoundland Nationalism

C Colleen O'Brien

D Political Science – UPO1107-01

E Professor Geoff Booth

F Friday, March 19, 2007

Colleen O'Brien Essay ©

Sample Essay

(K)

(G) NEWFOUNDLAND NATIONALISM   2

(H) We'll Rant and We'll Roar Like True Newfoundlanders:

(I) Newfoundland Nationalism

(J) A feeling of pride wells to the surface whenever a Newfoundlander speaks of home. Home is, of course, the rugged, craggy island of rock in the North Atlantic Ocean. But it is more than geography. Even if he or she has lived on the mainland of Canada most of his or her adult life, a Newfoundlander is just that: Newfoundlander first, Canadian second. More than just a regional identity, Newfoundlanders have a passionate sense of commonality that cannot be easily explained in words or understood by those who are not part of it. This sense of community has always fostered nationalism in Newfoundland, but there seems to be a new movement of nationalism sweeping its shores: it is a neo-nationalism led not by politicians, but by a new generation of islanders who are proud of their heritage and culture. In Hollywood movies, award-winning literature, popular music, and international media, Newfoundland culture is a hot commodity.

(J) Cultural nationalism is not a new phenomenon in Canadian politics. The rights revolution, as defined by Michael Ignatieff, is one of the many offspring born of a marital diversity in a political community known for its tolerance. The difficulty with this fractured version of Canadian politics is where we draw the line. Cultural nationalism is one thing, but to take that one step further in the form of civic nationalism, as the Quebec separatist movement has tried to do, is a maple leaf of a whole different colour. Canadian Aboriginals are identified and recognized as a distinct society, with special political provisions afforded them by law. Quebec is still fighting for preferential treatment by the federal government. In Newfoundland, the movement toward both civic nationalism and distinct status is gathering momentum and is the source of potential socioeconomic implications for the entire country of Canada.

(K)

Colleen O'Brien Essay ©

Sidebar callouts:

(G) Include a **running head** and **page number** on every page

(H) **Centre** the **title** and use mixed case

(I) **Double-space** between the **title** and the **first line** and all text

(J) **Tab** indent the first line of each paragraph

Use Times New Roman or a similar **font** and **12 point type**

(K) Leave one-inch **margins** (top, bottom, right, and left)

Sample Report

Use Times New Roman or similar **font** and 12 point type

(A) **Centre** the **title** and use **mixed case**

(B) **Double-space** between the title, the first line, and all text

(C) **Centre** and **bold first-level headings**

GREENING OF CANADIAN HOTEL INDUSTRY   2

(A) The Greening of the Canadian Hotel Industry

(B) In the 1990s, the North American hotel industry began responding to customers' demands for more environmentally friendly service. The need for waste reduction and recycling programs in an industry that routinely disposed of thousands of tonnes of plastics, paper, toiletries, water, and surplus food became increasingly obvious. Following the call to action by groups such as the Green Hotels Association ("Greening," 1998), travellers were encouraged to request green hotels for guest stays, meetings, conventions, and family events. Numerous hotels responded by lowering water and energy usage and by reducing solid waste. In Canada, many hotels and resorts have introduced green practices and offer a broad range of options for travellers. The purpose of this report is to explore the demand for greening, current conservation practices, specialized accommodations, and environmental education programs in Canadian hotels and resorts.

(C) **Discussion**

Today, it is relatively common to find towel and sheet-changing options, low-flow showers and toilets, soap and shampoo dispensers, and room recycling baskets. Frequently, hotel guests across North America now find signs displayed in their bathrooms stating, "Please decide for yourself. A towel on the rack means 'I'll use it several times.' A towel on the floor means 'Please exchange'" (Andrews, 1993, p. 22). Many hotels, however, have taken this movement . . .

Demand for Greening

In 1998, the U.S. Travel Data Center estimated that 43 million U.S. travellers were ecologically concerned ("Greening," 1998). In Canada, the situation is much the same...

GREENING OF CANADIAN HOTEL INDUSTRY   4   **D**

percent of their employees viewed the environment as a critical issue, 89 percent wanted to know more about what they could do to help, and 82 percent agreed to volunteer extra time and effort to help (Troyer, 1992). Together with government agencies and environmental groups, North American travellers and employees of the travel industry began agitating for recycling and waste-reduction programs. The Green Hotels Association distributed "The Meeting Planner's Questionnaire," urging conference planners to use this as a means of assessing the greenness of a hotel before booking accommodations. The questionnaire covered areas such as "recycling, purchasing of recycled or recyclable items, food and beverage service, bottle deposits, leftover food, meeting materials, guestroom amenities, guestroom linens, water and energy conservation" ("Green Hotels," 1997, p. 10). By choosing green hotels for meetings and convention sites, meeting planners began directly influencing the environmental awareness of the hotel industry. The success of the recent symposium held in Atlanta, Georgia, concerning the management of the supply and demand of environment-friendly hotels clearly indicates that the greening of hotels is seen by the industry as simply good for business. In Canada, the number of hotels . . .

F **Conservation Practices**

Canadian Pacific Hotels was the first major hotel chain in Canada to respond to the consumer demand for conservation. In Phase One of their "Green Partnership" corporate environmental program, CP Hotels placed blue recycling boxes in every one of its hotel rooms, made 90 percent of all used soap available to local charities, recycled 86 percent of all paper used in CP Hotels into paper that met or exceeded the Canadian Environmental Choice Standards, and reduced paper consumption by 20 percent in 80 percent of all CP Hotel properties (Jacquette, 1998). CP has also published *The CPH & R Green Partnership Guide* (1992), a handbook offering...

Place the **page number** **D** and **running head** on the same line

Leave **one-inch margins** (top, **E** bottom, right, and left)

Left justify and **bold second-level** **F** **headings**; use **mixed case**

Include a
running head
and **page
number** on
every page

(G)

Tab indent
the first line of
each paragraph

(H)

Do not start
a new page for
subsections
(e.g., Conclusion)

(I)

(G) GREENING OF CANADIAN HOTEL INDUSTRY   8

environmentally-friendly setting. CP Hotels' initiative was met by . . .

Specialized Accommodations

(H) While approximately 30 percent of all hotels in Canada today
provide recycling bins, refillable pump dispensers for amenities,
low-flow showerheads, faucet aerators and toilets, and energy-saving
lighting and heating systems, many hotels are moving toward providing
more comfortable environments for allergic and health-conscious
customers as well. Steve Belmonte, President and CEO of Ramada
Franchise Systems, noted that particular attention to "food-allergy safe"
practices in the preparation and service of food and beverages in hotels
is absolutely necessary to ensure not only the comfort but also the
safety of hotel guests (Marshall, 1995). . .

Environmental Education Programs

Phase Two of CP Hotels' corporate environmental program
is intended to move beyond the basics of recycling and energy
conservation. As Leslee Jaquette (1998) noted, according to
Environmental Affairs Supervisor Belinda Dusbaba, CP Hotels wants to
"'identify best practices, formalize corporate environmental practices
and motivate employees to continue to make positive changes at each
of our 26 properties'" (p. 32). The focus on incentive programs for
employees is perhaps the most innovative . . .

(I) Conclusion

This examination of the "greening" of the Canadian hotel industry
reveals both the success of current environmentally friendly practices
and educational programs – and the need for increased industry
incentives. While several hotels and lodging facilities have . . .

Sample Reference Page

Begin a new page for the list of references.

(A) GREENING OF CANADIAN HOTEL INDUSTRY   10

(B) References

(C) Andrews, J. (1993, November). Don't throw in the towel! *Environment, 35*(9), 22.

Cleaver, J. (1995). Allergy sufferers find peace, no pollen, in eco-friendly room. *Crain's Chicago Business, 18*(44).

F.L.C. (2000). Hoteliers and corporate travel buyers to promote "green" hotels together. *Cornell Hotel & Restaurant Administration Quarterly, 41*(5), 16.

Green Hotels Association offers Meeting Planner's Questionnaire. (1997, March/April). *Natural Life,* 10.

Greening your travel experience. (1998, December). *USA Today Magazine, 127*(2643), 15.

Holland, R. (1999). Company's products purify air, water in hotel rooms. *Boston Business Journal, 19*(19), 9.

Jacquette, L. (1998). Canadian Pacific renews environmental initiative. *Hotel & Motel Management, 213*(14), 32.   **(D)**

Marshall, A. (1995). Food allergies nothing to sneeze at. *Hotel & Motel Management, 210*(2), 11.

(E) Mulrine, A. (1999, October 18). Room service, send up a yogi: Hotels are introducing a wave of New Age perks aimed at business travelers. *U.S. News and World Report, 127*(15), 104.

Troyer, W. (1992). *The CPH & R green partnership guide: 12 steps to help create an environmentally-friendly setting for our guests, ourselves and our future.* Canada: Canadian Pacific Hotels & Resorts.

Include the **running head** and **page number**   **A**

Centre the word **"References"** at the top of the page   **B**

Set the **first line** of each entry **flush left** and **indent subsequent lines**   **C**

Double space all lines   **D**

List each entry **alphabetically** (according to the **first letter** of each entry)   **E**

"... maples turned scarlet across the pond, beneath where the white stems of three aspens diverged, at the point of a promontory, next to the water. Ah, many a tale their color told! And gradually from week to week the character of each tree came out, and it admired itself reflected in the smooth mirror of the lake. Each morning the manager of this gallery substituted some new picture, distinguished by more brilliant or harmonious coloring, for the old upon the walls."

Henry David Thoreau, 1849

3 Citing Sources

Citing Sources

You must acknowledge any ideas or facts used to write your paper by using in-text citations. In-text citations enclose in parentheses the author and date of any sources consulted in your research and page numbers for direct quotations.

IN-TEXT CITATIONS

An In-Text Citation:

1   Identifies your **research source** for a quotation or paraphrased information

2   **Leads readers** to the Reference list at the end of your paper for **further information** on the research source

TWO WAYS TO CITE

Direct Quotation:
Uses **exact words** from your source and always includes the source's page number

Paraphrase:
Uses your **own words to summarize** or **rephrase** the source's idea(s) and, depending on the discipline, may require page numbers

A CITATION

1   Follows an **idea or fact** taken from a research source

2   Includes (within parentheses) the **author's surname, publication date,** and, for direct quotations, **page number(s)**

3   Is normally **placed at the end of the sentence**. The punctuation for the sentence follows the citation.

Building a Citation

A citation acknowledges and documents the research source you used to emphasize, reinforce, or prove any point you made in your research paper.

If a source is in your Reference list, there must be an in-text citation for that source in your paper and vice versa. Research papers that do not cite sources could be liable for plagiarism! See pp. 5–7.

BASIC AUTHOR-DATE
A citation in APA style follows the author-date method.

(Author, Date)   (Wilson, 2008)

AUTHOR, NO DATE
If there is no date available for the citation, the abbreviation **n.d.** is used.

(Author, n.d.)   (Sanford, n.d.)

NO AUTHOR
If there is no author identified for the citation, use one or two keywords from the title followed by the year of publication. See the "No Author" example 5, *Section 4*.

(Title, Date)   ("Mugabe to Move," 2008)

DIRECT QUOTATION
The citation following a direct quotation must include the page reference.

(Author, Date, p. #)   (Wilson, 2008, p. 14)

ELECTRONIC SOURCES
Often electronic sources do not provide page numbers. In this case, use the paragraph number, if visible, preceded by "para." If neither paragraph nor page numbers are included, cite the heading (if lengthy, a shortened version) in quotation marks and provide a paragraph number within the section to direct the reader to the location of your source material.

(Author, Date, para. #)   (Statistics Canada, 2008, para. 1)

Using Direct Quotations

Work direct quotations into the grammatical structure and logic of your own sentences. Clearly **indicate the relevance** of the quoted material to your discussion. Never insert a quotation without an introduction.

Provide the **author's name, the publication year, and the page number** in an in-text citation directly following the quotation.

SHORT QUOTATIONS

Incorporate a short, direct quotation (fewer than 40 words) **directly into the text** of your paper and enclose it in **double quotation marks.** If you introduce the author in the text of your paper directly before the quotation, you do not need to include the author's name in your parenthetical citation (as in the second example).

Example 1

Confederation is still a sore issue with many Newfoundlanders. The campaign to join Canada was characterized as "the route a good Newfoundlander would take to benefit his people" (Thompson, 1980, p. 23).

Example 2

Confederation is still a sore issue with many Newfoundlanders. According to R.C. Thompson (1980), the campaign to join Canada was characterized as "the route a good Newfoundlander would take to benefit his people" (p. 23).

> **Note that the period *follows* the citation at the end of a short quotation.**

QUOTATION WITHIN A QUOTATION

Cite the source from which you are quoting. In the body of your paper, clearly state the author and work that your source text references. For example, to reference a quotation by Robert Allen quoted in a text on business communication by Locker, Kaczmarek, and Braun, cite Locker, Kaczmarek, and Braun as the authors, **not** Robert Allen.

Example

To argue the importance of developing excellent communications skills, the authors of *Business Communication: Building Critical Skills* include the comments of University of British Columbia economics professor, Robert Allen, from his study *Education and Technological Revolution: The Role of the Social Sciences and the Humanities in the Knowledge-based Economy.* According to Allen, "Demand is increasing for those workers who can . . . deal effectively with customers and other members of a team, speak and write clearly, and make informed and independent judgments" (Locker, Kaczmarek, & Braun, 2007, p. 23).

> **Note the use of double and single quotation marks.**

LONG QUOTATIONS

Set longer quotations (40 words or more) off from the rest of your written text by **block indenting** the quotation one tab from the left margin. Double-space the entire quotation and do not enclose it in quotation marks.

Example

A soaring increase in immune-related diseases such as rheumatoid arthritis, diabetes, lupus, allergies and asthma has encouraged doctors and scientists to look more seriously at the overcleanliness theory first advanced in 1989 by epidemiologist David Strachan:

> The "dirt" theory holds that immune systems learn to cope with the multitude of bacteria in filth and impure water from the moment of birth. The onslaught helps develop sophisticated immune cells, mostly in childhood. Without germs the immunity does not develop.
>
> An infant's immune system will become impaired if it is forced to grow in a sterile environment, says Graham Rook, an immunologist at University College London. John Fraser of the Auckland University School of Medicine says, "There is good scientific reason for believing that the fewer infectious diseases a person meets early in life, the more likely the immune system will be hypersensitive to allergens like pollens and dust mites." (Downey, 1999, p. 50)

> **Note that the period is placed before the in-text citation in a long quotation. Use double quotation marks, as in the example above, to indicate quoted material within your source quotation (quotation within a quotation).**

Paraphrasing

Paraphrasing an idea means putting the author's ideas into your own words.

WHEN PARAPHRASING, YOU MUST:

Include the author's name and the publication date in parentheses following the paraphrased material.

Some disciplines also require the page number of the text you are paraphrasing. Consult your instructor or professor.

PARAPHRASE

If you introduce the author in the text of your paper, you do not need to include the author's name in your reference (as in *Example 2*).

Example 1

In an unprecedented effort to address a shortage of skilled autoworkers, Ford Motor Co. of Canada donated $3 million to St. Clair College in Windsor, Ontario (Keenan, 2000).

Example 2

According to Greg Keenan (2000) of *The Globe and Mail*, Ford Motor Co. of Canada donated $3 million to St. Clair College in Windsor, Ontario, in an unprecedented effort to address a shortage of skilled autoworkers.

Example of Paraphrasing Within a Report or Research Paper

In 1998, the U.S. Travel Data Center estimated that 43 million U.S. travellers were ecologically concerned ("Greening," 1998). In Canada, the situation is much the same. According to a questionnaire distributed in 1992 by Canadian Pacific (CP) Hotels & Resorts, more than 95 percent of their employees viewed the environment as a critical issue, 89 percent wanted to know more about what they could do to help, and 82 percent agreed to volunteer extra time and effort to help (Troyer, 1992). . . .

Canadian Pacific Hotels was the first major hotel chain in Canada to respond to the consumer demand for conservation. In Phase One of their "Green Partnership" corporate environmental program, CP Hotels placed blue recycling boxes in every one of its hotel rooms, made 90 percent of all used soap available to local charities, recycled 86 percent of all paper used in CP Hotels into paper that met or exceeded the Canadian Environmental Choice Standards, and reduced paper consumption by 20 percent in 80 percent of all CP Hotel properties (Jacquette, 1998).

In-Text References to Books and Articles

The rules for CAPITALIZING and *italicizing* in the text or body of your report or essay are **different** from those you should follow for your citations (parenthetical information) and for your Reference list entries.

When you want to discuss a work in the body of your report, observe the following rules:

IN-TEXT REFERENCES TO BOOKS, FILMS, AND PERIODICALS (ENTIRE WORKS)

To refer to a book, film, or periodical (an entire magazine or newspaper), **CAPITALIZE** the first letter of each word in the title and **italicize** the title. Do not capitalize articles ("a" and "an"), prepositions ("in," "at," etc.), or conjunctions ("but," "and," "or") unless they are the first word of a title or follow a colon.

> Canadian Pacific Hotels has also published *The CPH & R Green Partnership Guide* (1992), a handbook offering practical advice to other hotels, institutions, and restaurants on how to create an environmentally-friendly setting.

IN-TEXT REFERENCES TO ARTICLES AND CHAPTERS

To refer to an article or chapter from a book or periodical, **CAPITALIZE** the **first letter** of each word in the **title** and place the title in **quotation marks**.

> Leslee Jaquette's article, "Canadian Pacific Renews Environmental Initiative" (1998), outlines Phase Two of CP Hotel's corporate environmental program.

Photo © Heather Holm

"That whimsical fellow called Evolution, having enlarged the dinosaur until he tripped over his own toes, tried shrinking the chickadee until he was just too big to be snapped up by flycatchers as an insect, and just too little to be pursued by hawks and owls as meat."

Aldo Leopold, 1949

Using
In-Text Citations

4

Using In-Text Citations

APA format requires the author-date method of citation. Periods, commas, and semicolons are placed **outside** the citation. The following lists some guidelines and examples.

ARTICLES IN BOOKS OR PERIODICALS

ELECTRONIC SOURCES

OTHER PUBLICATIONS

Articles in Books or Periodicals

Magazines, journals, and newspapers are considered "**periodicals.**" The following examples show how to cite references to ideas and facts from books and/or periodicals.

1 SINGLE AUTHOR

Cite the **author's surname**, the **date of publication**, and **page number** (if a quotation is used).

One of the founders of Canada's Confederation, D'Arcy McGee was known as a man of extremes whose "powerful passions were in a state of creative tension with his impressive intellect" (Wilson, 2008, p.14).

A talented journalist and orator as well as one of Canada's founders, D'Arcy McGee was a man of intelligence and passion (Wilson, 2008).

2 SINGLE AUTHOR (SIGNAL PHRASE)

If you indicate the author's name in the body of your sentence, cite only the **date of publication**:

Biographer David Wilson (2008) describes D'Arcy McGee as a man of intelligence and many passions.

3 MULTIPLE WORKS BY ONE AUTHOR

List multiple works by one author within a single set of parentheses in **chronological order.**

Northrop Frye's numerous publications on education reflect his lifelong commitment to the value of teaching literature (Frye, 1963, 1967, 1988, 1990).

4 MULTIPLE WORKS BY ONE AUTHOR WITH THE SAME DATE

Use **suffixes** (a, b, c, and so on) to identify **multiple works by one author** published in the same year. In the References list, order these works **alphabetically by title, and include the particular suffix assigned to the year**.

That year he published several studies on education as well as literary criticism (Frye, 1963a, 1963b, 1963c).

5   NO AUTHOR

Use one or two **key words from the title** followed by the **year of publication**. Use double quotation marks around the title of an article or chapter. For example, for an article titled "Mugabe to Move Swiftly After Vote," use "Mugabe to Move."

Zimbabwe is currently a country in turmoil with both the opposition and ruling party, led by Mugabe, claiming victory in the recent election. To restore order, the opposition has "called for the deployment of thousands of African Union peacekeeping troops to bring order to a nation ravaged by months of political violence" ("Mugabe to Move," 2008, p. AA2).

6   TWO AUTHORS

Cite **both authors' surnames** joined by an "**&**":

A recent study discusses the role of imaginary friends in the development of communication skills in children aged four to six (Roby & Kidd, 2008).

7   THREE TO FIVE AUTHORS

Cite all the **authors' surnames in the first reference**; for subsequent references include only the **surname of the first author** followed by "**et al.**" and the year. **Subsequent references:** (Guffey et al., 2006)

Clarity and conciseness are two major principles of effective business writing (Guffey, Rhodes, & Rogin, 2006).

8   SIX OR MORE AUTHORS

Cite only the **surname of the first author** followed by "**et al.**" and the year for first and subsequent references: (Taylor et al., 2008)

9   TWO OR MORE WORKS BY DIFFERENT AUTHORS

To cite several studies by different authors, cite the **authors' names in alphabetical order** inside **one set of parentheses**. Separate the citations by **semicolons**.

Numerous articles (Cleaver, 1995; Holland, 1999; Marshall, 1995) suggest that the "green" movement of the hotel industry has gone beyond the "reduce, re-use, recycle" environmental golden rule.

10 GROUP OR CORPORATE AUTHOR

Groups as authors include corporations, businesses, associations, government agencies, and study groups. Cite the name of the group in the first reference and include the acronym in square brackets for the group. Subsequent references may be abbreviated as indicated in the initial citation: (CAW, n.d.)

The union for auto workers made clear their position that climate change is "serious" and "global action" is necessary (Canadian Auto Workers, [CAW], n.d.).

11 SPECIFIC PARTS OF A SOURCE

To cite a part of a work, indicate the **chapter, figure, table**, or **equation**.

This section of her study provides an excellent discussion of recent student and community action against the brand bullies (Klein, 2000, Chapter 17).

12 WORK DISCUSSED IN A SECONDARY SOURCE

Cite the source text of your reference or the source from which you are quoting. In the body of your paper, clearly state the **author and work** that your source text references. For example, to refer to an idea or fact from a book written by Katz discussed in an article written by Jones, cite Jones, not Katz as your source.

As Jones discusses, Katz's study indicated that, historically, ideals of beauty have had a negative impact on women's health (Jones, 2000).

In Katz's study of teenaged girls' eating disorders he concluded that "myths of femininity largely function to disable women's health and well-being" (as cited in Jones, 2000, p. 89).

Note the use of "as cited in" in the example above of a direct quotation taken from another source.

13 QUOTATION WITHIN A QUOTATION

Use **single quotation marks** within double quotation marks to indicate material quoted in a source text (quotation within a quotation). Cite the source in which you found the information — not the original work.

The Globe and Mail recently reported a recall of the drug heparin. A spokesperson for the company involved announced that "patients who have the product 'should discontinue use immediately,' but added that the product is used almost exclusively in hospitals" (Picard, 2008, p. A9).

14 CLASSIC WORKS

When citing old works, cite both the **original publication date** and the **date of your version**. For a work by Shelley, originally published in 1818 and republished in 2000, the citation is (Shelley, 1818/2000).

For very old works for which the date of publication is unavailable, cite the **year of the translation** you used, preceded by "**trans.**" or the year of the version you used followed by "**version.**"

For example:
(Plato, trans. 1955).

15 PARTS OF CLASSIC WORKS

Refer to parts of major classical works (Greek and Roman works, the Bible, Shakespeare, and so on) in the text of your paper by part (e.g., books, chapters, verses, lines, cantos).

For example:
Following a quotation of lines 129 and 130 in Act 1, Scene 2 of William Shakespeare's *Hamlet*, cite the following: (1.2.129-130)

Electronic Sources

Use the same format to cite electronic sources as you would to cite a print source. (See *Building a Citation, Section 3,* p. 21)

If an electronic document does not indicate the name of the author(s), place in the author position either a **shortened version of the title** or the **name of the organization** that published the document. Readers will know to look in the *References* page under the term chosen in place of the author.

---

16 SINGLE AUTHOR

Cite the **author's surname** and the **date of publication** or **update** or the **date of retrieval**.

Provincial and federal governments have recognized the importance of global warming on the national economy (Sanford, 2008).

17 NO DATE

Write "**n.d.**" if there is no date of publication.

Sound quality is affected by both the audio equipment and the interior's architectural design (Haas, n.d.).

18 NO AUTHOR

If no individual author of a Web site document is indicated, cite either the **name of the organization, group, or Web site publisher** or a **shortened version of the title.**

Fertilizer run-off has been cited as a concern at the global level ("World Flips," 2008).

Inuit children were found to be active in sports 10% more than non-Inuit Canadian children (Statistics Canada, 2008, para. 1).

19 MULTIPLE AUTHORS

Follow the same directions as those for citing multiple authors in books and periodicals (see pp. 29-31).

A recent major study conducted by the Psychology Department at the University of Missouri-Columbia showed that real-life violent video game play increases aggressive behaviour and delinquency (Anderson & Dill, 2000).

Other Publications

20 COMIC STRIP, PHOTOGRAPH, OR ILLUSTRATION

Cite the source of the comic strip, photograph, or illustration according to the **correct format** for that source.

Dilbert characters reveal the power dynamics that exist within mentoring relationships (Adams, 2002).

Although best known for his abstracts, he ventures into realism in his most recent portraits of some of his painting peers (Rayner, 2001).

Note the References list entries in *Section 6*, examples 29 and 40.

21 DICTIONARY/ENCYCLOPEDIA DEFINITION

If the entry is unsigned (no author), use a **shortened version of the title of the entry** from the dictionary or encyclopedia in place of the author's name.

Embryology is defined as "the study of the origin, growth, development and function of an organism from fertilization to birth" ("Embryology," 2006, p. 631).

22 PERSONAL COMMUNICATION

Personal communication includes **interviews, lectures, telephone conversations, letters, and memos.** Give the **initials as well as the surname** of the communicator. Do not include personal communications in your References list **unless retrieved from an online source.**

As a registered massage therapist explained, "Therapeutic massage is an important part of our health care and is playing an ever-increasing role in the improvement of people's health" (K. Mackay, personal communication, June 9, 2008).

Photo © Heather Holm

"...I happened to look down to the mossy shelf below and there in the shade made the discovery of the day, a single pink lady-slipper in full bloom. While I looked at it, I forgot the heat and humidity and thought of the great woods to the south where its closest kin, the showy lady-slipper is found, and of all the great solitudes of the earth where members of the orchis family bloom. Alike in their needs, no matter where they grow, in the depths of tropical jungles or in the woods of the north, shadows and solitudes are part of their lives. They are flowers of primeval and the unchanged places of the earth."

Sigurd F. Olson, 1958

5 Preparing Your Reference List

Preparing Your Reference List

The last page of your research paper is the *References* page in which you list **all of the sources cited** within the text of your paper.

Do not include materials consulted in your research that were not directly cited in your paper.

REFERENCE ENTRIES FOR ONLINE SOURCES

The sixth edition of the *Publication Manual of the American Psychological Association* includes new simplified guidelines for citing online sources. In general, the new guidelines for online sources follow the format for fixed media references.

A **Digital Object Identifier** (DOI) is an alphanumeric code for both print and online articles and materials, e.g., DOI:10.1016j.bbi2007.12.002. It acts as a fixed identifier/link to scholarly content. **No further retrieval information is required if a DOI is available.**

DOIs are usually found on the first page of a document such as a PDF file. Some databases may hide the DOI behind a button marked "Article" or "PubMed." CrossRef.org is a web site that provides a link resolver for finding material through a DOI.

Include the DOI, if available, for both print and online articles.

When a DOI is not available, include the home page URL, e.g.,
    Retrieved from http://www.canadianart.ca

Because of the complexity of a DOI, it is best to copy and paste it into the reference list. In the reference entry, use lower case letters for "DOI" as in the example below.

Example: Article with a Digital Object Identifier (DOI)

Fishbach, A., & Labroo, A. (2007). Be better or be merry: How mood affects self-control. *Journal of Personality and Social Psychology,* *93*(2), 158-173. doi:10.1037/0022-3514.93.2.158

Example: Article with No Digital Object Identifier (DOI)

Jager, D. (2009, September 1). Kelly Richardson: The radiant real. Retrieved from http://www.canadianart.ca

Example: Article from a Database (NO DOI) NEW

Lertzman, D.A., & Vredenburg, H. (2005, February). Indigenous peoples, resource extraction and sustainable development: An ethical approach. *Journal of Business Ethics*, *56*(3), 239-254. Retrieved from http://www.philinfo.org.

If a journal article has no DOI and is retrieved from a library database, complete a Web search to find the home page URL of the journal.

Building a Reference Entry

Think of each part of a reference entry as a unit. Each **unit** is **separated by a period.**

BOOK					
Author.	(Date).	*Title.*	Location:	Publisher.	

Hage, R. (2006). *DeNiro's game.* Toronto: Anansi.

PERIODICAL					
Author.	(Date).	Title of Article.	*Title of Periodical,*	*Volume*(Issue),	Page(s).

Diedrich, R. C. (2008). Still more about coaching! *Consulting Psychology Journal: Practice and Research, 60*(1), 4-6. doi:10.1037/1065-9293.60.1.4

PERIODICAL (NO AUTHOR)				
Title of Article.	(Date).	*Title of Periodical,*	*Volume*(Issue),	Page(s).

Preview: A cross-Canada guide to the season's best exhibitions and events in the visual arts. (2007). *Canadian Art, 24*(4), 20-31.

ELECTRONIC ENTRIES

JOURNAL ARTICLE (WITH DOI)						
Author.	(Date).	Title of Article.	*Title of Periodical,*	*Volume*(Issue),	Page(s).	DOI

Fishbach, A., & Labroo, A. (2007). Be better or be merry: How mood affects self-control. *Journal of Personality and Social Psychology, 93*(2), 158–173. doi:10.1037/0022-3514.93.2.158

JOURNAL ARTICLE FROM A DATABASE (NO DOI)						
Author.	(Date).	Title of Article.	*Title of Periodical,*	*Volume*(Issue),	Page(s).	Retrieval Statement

Sanford, J. (2008, July 21). A tangled web. *Canadian Business, 81*(11), 16. Retrieved from http://www.canadianbusiness.com

ONLINE JOURNAL ARTICLE (NO DOI)						
Author.	(Date).	Title of Article.	*Title of Periodical,*	*Volume*(Issue),	Page(s).	Retrieval Statement

Dalle, S. P., & De Blois, S. (2006). Shorter fallow cycles affect the availability of noncrop plant resources in a shifting cultivation system. *Ecology and Society, 11*(2), 2. Retrieved from http://www.ecologyandsociety.org/vol11/iss2/art2/

Setting up a Reference Page

A List entries alphabetically

B Set the first line of each entry flush left and indent subsequent lines

C Use "&" to join the surnames of the last two authors

D Capitalize the first letter only of the title of an article

E Include the issue number in parentheses immediately following the volume number for all online journals

F Include the Digital Object Identifier (DOI) when provided

G Use (n.d.) if there is no date of publication

H Capitalize the first letter of a word that follows a colon

I When the author and the publisher are the same, use "Author" as the publisher

CITES & SOURCES   15

References

A Athabasca University. (n.d.). *The AU library guide to*

B *the research process.* Retrieved from

http://.library.athabascau.ca/help/guide/

guide2research.html

Buske-Kirschbaum, A., Ebrecht, M., Kern, S., Gierens, A.,

C & Hellhammer, D. H. (2008). **D** Personality

characteristics in chronic and non-chronic allergic

conditions. *Brain, Behavior & Immunity, 22*(5), **E**

762-768. **F** doi:10.1016/j.bbi.2007.12.002

Canadian Auto Workers. **G** (n.d.). *Climate change and*

our jobs: **H** *Finding the right balance.* Toronto: Author. **I**

J For entries that begin with "A, "An," or "The," alphabetize by the first letter of the second word

K Capitalize the first letter only of a non-periodical (books, brochures, Web documents, audio-visual productions)

L Enclose non-routine information in square brackets immediately after the title and before the period

M Capitalize the titles of periodicals (newspapers, journals, magazines, scholarly newsletters)

J The Law Society of Upper Canada. (n.d.). **K** *Looking for a lawyer?* **L** [Brochure].

Picard, A. (2008, March 25). Recall issued for heparin marketed in Canada. **M** *The Globe and Mail,* **N** p. A9.

O Preview: A cross-Canada guide to the season's best exhibitions and events in the visual arts. (2007). *Canadian Art, 2* **P** (4), 20-31.

Roby, A. C., & Kidd, E. (2008, July). The referential communication skills of children with imaginary companions. **Q** *Developmental Science,* **R** *11,* **S** 531-540. doi:10.1111/j.1467-7687.2008.00699

N Use "p." or "pp." for books, newspaper articles, and works in anthologies

O For an entry with no author or editor, move the title to the author position

P Include the issue number in parentheses immediately following the volume number of a journal that begins each issue with page 1

Q Italicize the titles of print, audiovisual, and online works (books, journals, newspapers, magazines, reports, Web documents, brochures, films, videos, and television and radio productions)

R Italicize volume numbers and do not use "Vol." before the number

S Do not use "p." or "pp." for articles in magazines or scholarly journals

General Formatting Rules

Formatting References list entries according to APA-style documentation rules requires **close attention to detail**.

The following rules provide the general guidelines. For examples of the most common sources that writers and students use as references, see *Section 6: Reference List Entries*.

ORDER OF REFERENCES

1 ALPHABETICAL ORDER
List entries alphabetically by surname of the first author:

Francis, R. D., Jones, R., & Smith, D. B. (2006). *Journeys: A history of Canada.*
    Toronto: Nelson.

Payton, B. (2008, March). Fat of the land. *The Walrus, 5*, 46-53.

2 NO AUTHOR OR NO EDITOR
Move the title to the author position and list alphabetically by the first word of the title:

Mugabe to move swiftly after vote. (2008, June 26). *The Toronto Star*, pp. AA1-2.

Phipps, J. J. (2005). E-Journaling: Achieving interactive education online.
    Educause Quarterly 28(1). Retrieved from http://connect.educause.edu/Library/
    EDUCAUSE+Quarterly/EJournalingAchievingInter/39909

3 NO AUTHOR, TITLE BEGINNING WITH "THE," "A," OR "AN"
List according to the first letter of the word immediately following "The," "A," or "An":

The Doubleday Roget's thesaurus in dictionary form.
An odyssey of Canadian verse.

4 MULTIPLE ENTRIES BY SAME AUTHOR
List by year of publication, earliest first:

Freud, S. (1900).
Freud, S. (1915).

5 SAME AUTHOR, SAME PUBLICATION DATE
Arrange alphabetically by title and include the suffix (a, b, c, and so on) assigned to the year in the in-text citation:

Frye, N. (1963a). The educated imagination.

Frye, N. (1963b). Fables of identity.

Frye, N. (1963c). The well-tempered critic.

6 DIFFERENT AUTHORS, SAME SURNAME
Arrange alphabetically by the first initial:

Hamilton, H.
Hamilton, J.

7 GROUP AUTHORS (ASSOCIATIONS, GOVERNMENT AGENCIES)
List by the first word of the name of the association:

Community Legal Education Ontario.

Statistics Canada.

CAPITALIZATION

1 TITLE OF AN ARTICLE OR CHAPTER
Capitalize the first letter only of the title:

Diedrich, R. C. (2008). Still more about coaching! *Consulting Psychology Journal: Practice and Research, 60*(1), 4-6.

2 TITLE OF NON-PERIODICALS
(BOOKS, BROCHURES, WEB DOCUMENTS, AUDIO-VISUAL PRODUCTIONS)
Capitalize only the title's first letter:

The Law Society of Upper Canada. (n.d.). *Looking for a lawyer?* [Brochure].

3 PERIODICALS
(NEWSPAPERS, JOURNALS, MAGAZINES, SCHOLARLY NEWSLETTERS)
Capitalize the title:

Columbia's resurgence. (2008, July 4). [Editorial]. *The Globe and Mail,* p. A14.

4 WORD FOLLOWING A COLON
Capitalize the first letter:

Alzheimer Society of Canada, (2000). *Alzheimer disease: A handbook for care* [Brochure].

5 IN-TEXT CITATION WITH TITLE IN PLACE OF AUTHOR
Capitalize the first letter of each word:

Zimbabwe is currently in a state of turmoil with the opposition party calling for aid from other African countries ("Mugabe to Move," 2008).

6 IN-TEXT REFERENCE TO TITLE OF ENTIRE WORK
Capitalize the first letter of each word:

Many of these approaches are outlined in *Alzheimer Disease: A Handbook for Care* (Alzheimer Society of Canada, 2000).

7 IN-TEXT REFERENCE TO TITLE OF AN ARTICLE OR CHAPTER
Capitalize the first letter of each word:

Leslee Jaquette's article, "Canadian Pacific Renews Environmental Initiative" (1998), outlines Phase Two of CP Hotel's corporate environmental program.

ITALICS

1 TITLES OF PRINT, AUDIOVISUAL, AND ONLINE WORKS
Italicize the titles of books, journals, newspapers, magazines, reports, Web documents, brochures, films, videos, and television and radio productions:

Gunnarsson, S. (Director). (2008). *Air India 182* [Motion picture]. Canada: 52 Media/ Eurasia Motion Pictures Inc.

2 VOLUME NUMBERS OF JOURNALS
Italicize the volume numbers:

Szewczyk, M. (2007). Footnotes from Moscow. *Canadian Art, 24*(3), 98-101.

3 TITLES OF PRINT, AUDIOVISUAL, AND ONLINE WORKS
Italicize the titles of books, journals, newspapers, videos, etc. when referred to in-text:

Canadian Pacific Hotels has also published *The CPH & Green Partnership Guide* (1992), a handbook offering practical advice to other hotels, institutions and restaurants on how to create an environmentally friendly setting.

PARENTHESES

1 DATE OF PUBLICATION

Enclose the date of publication in parentheses:

Honda Motor Co. Ltd. (2007). *Annual Report 2007.* Retrieved from http://world.honda.
com/investors/annualreport/2007/pdf/ar2007.pdf

2 JOURNAL ARTICLES WITH ISSUE NUMBER

For journals that begin each issue with page 1, enclose the issue number in parentheses immediately following the volume number:

Diedrich, R. C. (2008). Still more about coaching! *Consulting Psychology
Journal: Practice and Research, 60*(1), 4-6. doi:10.1037/1065-9293.60.1.4

3 ONLINE JOURNALS

For all journal articles retrieved online, enclose the issue number in parentheses immediately following the volume number:

Van Eijck, M., & Roth, W. M. (2007). Improving science education for sustainable
development. *PloS Biology, 5*(12). doi:10.1371/journalpbio.0050306

4 SQUARE BRACKETS FOR NON-ROUTINE INFORMATION

Use square brackets immediately after the title and before the period to enclose non-routine information:

Héber, P. (2008). The need for an institute of continuing health education [Editorial].
Canadian Medical Association Journal, 178, 805-810. doi:10.1503/cmaj.080317

PAGINATION

1 ARTICLES OR CHAPTERS IN BOOKS, NEWSPAPERS, AND ANTHOLOGIES
Use "p." or "pp." to reference articles or chapters in books, newspapers, and anthologies:

Johnson, P. (2007). A Squamish legend of Napoleon. In S. Kamboureli (Ed.),
Making a difference (pp. 13-16). Don Mills, ON: Oxford University Press.

Picard, A. (2008, March 25). Recall issued for heparin marketed in Canada. *The Globe and Mail*, p. A9.

2 ARTICLES IN MAGAZINES OR SCHOLARLY JOURNALS
Do not use "p." or "pp." to reference articles in magazines or scholarly journals:

Szewczyk, M. (2007). Footnotes from Moscow. *Canadian Art, 24*(3), 98-101.

DATE OF PUBLICATION

1 Give the **date of publication** in **parentheses**.

2 For **unpublished works**, give the **year** the work was **produced**.

3 For **Internet sources**, see *Section 5*, pp. 38-39.

4 For **newspapers, journals, magazines, and newletters,** use the following formats:

Dailies and weeklies: (2007, December 14).

Journals: (2008).

Monthly magazines and newsletters: (2006, October)

Bimonthly magazines and newsletters: (2005, March/April).

Magazines and newsletters published quarterly or biannually: (2001, Spring).

Work with no date available: (n.d.).

Work accepted for publication but not yet printed: (in press).

PLACE OF PUBLICATION

1 Include the **place of publication** for all **nonperiodicals** (books and audio-visual productions).

2 **Do not include** the **place of publication** for **periodicals** (newspapers, journals, magazines, scholarly newsletters).

3 List the **place of publication** as the **city** followed by the abbreviation for the **state or province**, and the name of the **country** if the publisher is outside North America. Use the Canada Post abbreviations for the names of the provinces and states (e.g., ON for Ontario).

4 The following **locations** can be **listed without a state or country** abbreviation because they are well known for publishing: *Toronto, Amsterdam, Baltimore, Boston, Chicago, Los Angeles, New York, Philadelphia, San Francisco, Jerusalem, London, Milan, Moscow, Paris, Rome, Stockholm, Tokyo, and Vienna.*

PUBLISHER

1 Give the **name of the publisher** in as **brief** a form as possible. Omit terms such as *Publishers, Co., or Inc.,* but include *Press.*

2 When **two or more publisher locations** are given, give the **location listed first** in the book or, if specified, the location of the pubisher's home office.

"I never feel the soul of the plains express their quiet and peaceful beauty in a more inspiring way than when I stand on one of the bluffs of a river, looking out over the vast prairies at sunset time with the purple horizon as the background."

Jens Jensen, 1939

6 Reference List Entries

Reference List Entries

The following list provides examples of the most common sources that writers and students use as references.

The sample Reference list items will show you in what order to present **bibliographical information** (author, date, title, publisher) and when to use *italics*, CAPITALS, periods, spaces, etc., to format your entries.

For each type of reference entry (book, magazine, film, etc.), **follow the format of the example exactly as printed, especially if you are using citation software.** If you use a reference source not listed here, refer to the latest edition of the Publication Manual of the American Psychological Association.

You can also visit the APA Web site at **http://www.apastyle.org** The site provides format suggestions and examples.

ARTICLES IN BOOKS OR PERIODICALS

1   Article in a Magazine or Journal

2   Article in a Magazine or Journal (Two to Seven Authors)

3   Article in a Magazine or Journal (Eight or More Authors)

4   Article in a Magazine or Journal (No Author)

5   Article in a Magazine or Journal (Volume and Issue)

6   Article in a Magazine or Journal (Special Issue)

7   Article in a Newspaper

8   Article in a Newspaper (No Author)

9   Article/Chapter in an Edited Book or Anthology

10 Article/Chapter in a Multivolume Book

11 Editorial

12 Editorial (No Author)

13 Introduction/Foreword/Preface/ Afterword

14 Letter to the Editor

15 Review of a Book/Film/Performance

BOOKS AND BROCHURES

16 Book by One Author

17 Book by Two or More Authors

18 Book by Translator

19 Book in Multiple Volumes

20 Book in Republished Edition

21 Book in Second and Subsequent Editions

22 Book with an Author and Editor

23 Book/Textbook by Editor

24 Brochure

25 Brochure (No Date)

26 Classical Works

27 Government Document

28 Group or Corporate Authors

OTHER PUBLICATIONS

ELECTRONIC SOURCES

Articles in Books or Periodicals

1   **Article in a Magazine or Journal**

Payton, B. (2008, March). Fat of the land. *The Walrus, 5,*
46-53.

 2   **Article in a Magazine or Journal (Two to Seven Authors)**

Roby, A. C., & Kidd, E. (2008, July). The referential
communication skills of children with imaginary
companions. *Developmental Science, 11,* 531-540.
doi:10.1111/j.1467-7687.2008.00699

**For two to seven authors, include all names. If
a print article has a DOI, include it in the
reference entry.**

 3   **Article in a Magazine or Journal (Eight or More Authors)**

Sharma, K. C., Singh, H., Gupta, V., Mishra, V., Mittal,
M. K., Muraka, A.,... Jha, D. (2008). Giant cervical
lipoma with cervicomedullary epidural extension.
Pediatric Neurosurgery, 44, 258-260.
doi:10.1159/000121476

**Include the first six authors, followed by ellipsis,
then the last author.**

4   **Article in a Magazine or Journal (No Author)**

Preview: A cross-Canada guide to the season's best
exhibitions and events in the visual arts. (2007).
Canadian Art, 24(4), 20-31.

5 Article in a Magazine or Journal (Volume and Issue)

Diedrich, R. C. (2008). Still more about coaching!
*Consulting Psychology Journal: Practice and
Research*, 60(1), 4-6. doi:10.1037/1065-9293.60.1.4

**With journals that begin each issue with page 1, the
issue number is placed in parentheses immediately
following the volume number with no space between.**

6 Article in a Magazine or Journal (Special Issue)

Schalge, S. L., & Rudolph, C. E. (2007). Race as cultural
construction, race as social reality: Mothering
for contradictions and ambiguities [Special issue:
Mothering, race, ethnicity, culture and class]. *Journal
of the Association for Research on Mothering, 9*, 9-19.

**Use square brackets to include non-routine information
such as the title of a special issue or edition.**

7 Article in a Newspaper

Picard, A. (2008, March 25). Recall issued for heparin
marketed in Canada. *The Globe and Mail*, p. A9.

8 Article in a Newspaper (No Author)

Mugabe to move swiftly after vote. (2008, June 26). *The
Toronto Star*, pp. AA1-2.

**When no author is given, simply place the title in the
author position.**

9 Article/Chapter in an Edited Book or Anthology

Johnson, P. (2007). A Squamish legend of Napoleon. In
S. Kamboureli (Ed.), *Making a difference* (pp. 13-16).
Don Mills, ON: Oxford University Press.

10 **Article/Chapter in a Multivolume Book**

Wilson, D. A. (2008). A false sense of honour: June - September, 1848. In *Thomas D'Arcy McGee: Passion, reason, and politics*. (Vol. 1, pp. 203-223). Montreal, QC: McGill-Queen's University Press.

11 **Editorial**

Héber, P. (2008). The need for an institute of continuing health education [Editorial]. *Canadian Medical Association Journal, 178*, 805-810. doi:10.1503/cmaj.080317

12 **Editorial (No Author)**

Colombia's resurgence. (2008, July 4). [Editorial]. *The Globe and Mail*, p. A14.

When an editorial is unsigned (no author), begin the entry with the title of the editorial.

13 **Introduction/Foreword/Preface/Afterword**

Walker, N. A. (2000). Introduction: Biographical and historical contexts. In K. Chopin, *The Awakening* (2nd ed., pp. 3-21). Boston: Bedford/St. Martin's.

14 **Letter to the Editor**

Murphy, E. (2008, July/August). Freezing garlic [Letter to the editor]. *Cook's Illustrated*, p. 2.

NEW **15** **Review of a Book/Film/Performance**

Thomas, C. (2008, January/February). Unearthing a part of the underground railroad [Review of the book *I've got a home in glory land: The lost tale of the underground railroad,* by K. Smardz-Frost]. *Books in Canada, 37*(1), 13-14.

Use the reviewer's name as the author.

Books and Brochures

16 **Book by One Author**

Hage, R. (2006). *DeNiro's game*. Toronto: Anansi.

17 **Book by Two or More Authors**

Novak, M., & Campbell, L. (2006). *Aging and society: A Canadian perspective* (5th ed.). Scarborough, ON: Nelson.

Francis, R. D., Jones, R., & Smith, D. B. (2006). *Journeys: A history of Canada*. Toronto: Nelson.

For seven or more authors, list the first six and indicate the remaining with "et al."

18 **Book by Translator**

Nemirovsky, I. (2006). *Suite française* (S. Smith, Trans.). New York: Knopf. (Original work published 2004)

19 **Book in Multiple Volumes**

Wilson, D. A. (2008). *Thomas D'Arcy McGee: Passion, reason, and politics, 1825-1857* (Vol. 1). Montreal, QC: McGill-Queen's University Press.

20 **Book in Republished Edition**

Agamben, G. (2007). *The coming community* (M. Hardt, Trans.). Minneapolis, MN: University of Minnesota Press. (Original work published 1993)

21 **Book in Second and Subsequent Editions**

Guffey, M. E., Rhodes, K., & Rogin, P. (2006). *Business communication: Process and product* (5th Canadian ed.). Scarborough, ON: Nelson.

22 **Book with an Author and Editor**

Shelley, M. (2000). *Frankenstein* (2nd ed., J. M. Smith, Ed.). Boston: Bedford-St. Martin's. (Original work published 1818)

23 **Book/Textbook by Editor**

Barnet, S., Berman, M., Burto, W., Cain, W. E., & Stubbs, M. (Eds.). (2000). *Literature for composition: Essays, fiction, poetry, and drama* (5th ed.). New York: Longman.

24 **Brochure**

Community Legal Education Ontario. (2007, December). *Do you know a woman who is being abused?* [Brochure].

25 **Brochure (No Date)**

The Law Society of Upper Canada. (n.d.). *Looking for a lawyer?* [Brochure].

26 **Classical Works**

Classical works such as ancient Greek works and the Bible are not listed in your References list. Refer to them by part in the text of your paper (e.g., books, chapters, verses, lines, cantos). Identify the version in the first citation. For example: 1 Cor. 131:1 (Revised Standard Version).

27 **Government Document**

Statistics Canada. (2005). Population projections for Canada, provinces and territories 2005-2031 (91-520-XPE). Ottawa, ON: Ministry of Industry.

28 **Group or Corporate Authors**

Canadian Auto Workers. (n.d.). *Climate change and our jobs: Finding the right balance.* Toronto: Author.

When the author is a group or corporation, the publisher is often the same organization. In this case, give the publisher's name as "Author."

Other Publications

29   **Comic Strip**

Adams, S. (2002, June 15). Dilbert [Comic Strip]. *The Toronto Star*, p. R1.

30   **Entry in an Atlas**

Bertaux, J. L. (1996). Comets. In J. Audouze & G. Israel (Eds.). *The Cambridge atlas of astronomy* (3rd ed., pp. 234-237). Cambridge: Cambridge University Press.

31   **Encyclopedia/Dictionary**

Porteus, A. (2000). *Dictionary of environmental science and technology.* Chichester, NY: J. Wiley.

Onions, C., et al. (Ed.). (1971). *The compact edition of the Oxford English dictionary* (Vols. 1-2). Glasgow, Scotland: Oxford University Press.

32   **Entry in an Encyclopedia/Dictionary**

Pratt, R. (1999). Phoenix. In *Encyclopedia of Greek mythology* (Vol. 3, pp. 521-522). Oxford: Oxford University Press.

33   **Entry in an Encyclopedia/Dictionary (No Author)**

Embryology. (2006). *Mosby's medical dictionary* (7th ed.). St. Louis, MO: Mosby.

When no author is given, simply place the title of the entry in the author position.

34   **Film**

Gunnarsson, S. (Director). (2008). *Air India 182* [Motion picture]. Canada: 52 Media/Eurasia Motion Pictures Inc.

35 Music Recording

Lennon, J., & McCartney, P. (1965). In my life. On *Rubber soul* [Record]. London: Capitol.

36 Media Release

Office of Aileen Carroll, MPP Barrie. (2008, June 20). *Millions in new and innovative community programming part of historic Aging at Home strategy* [Media release].

37 Television Broadcast

Whitten, J. (Executive Producer). (2008, April 19). *Mansbridge one on one* [Television broadcast]. Toronto: CBC.

38 Unpublished Paper Presented in a Meeting

Vardalos, M. (2008, May). *Terrorized by melancholy: The science of depression and the production of the happy consciousness.* Paper presented at The Human Condition Series Conference, Georgian College, Barrie, ON.

39 Video

Lam, M. (Director/Researcher), Lynch, T., & Barrie, A. M. (Producers). (1998). *Show girls: Celebrating Montreal's legendary black jazz scene* [Video]. Canada: National Film Board of Canada.

40 Work of Art

Andrews, S. (2008). *Crowd* [Painting]. *Canadian Art, 24*(4), 40.

Harris, L. S. (1917). *Snow* [Painting]. McMichael Canadian Art Collection, Kleinburg, Ontario.

Name the gallery or institution that houses the piece. If you refer to a photograph of a work, include the source of the reproduction in your entry as in the first sample above.

Electronic Sources

New APA rules for citing electronic sources are included in the following examples of Reference list entries.

41 Annual Corporate Report

Honda Motor Co. Ltd. (2007). *Annual report 2007.* Retrieved from http://world.honda.com/investors/ annualreport/2007/pdf/ar2007.pdf

42 Article from a Web Site

Athabasca University. (n.d.). *The AU library guide to the research process.* Retrieved from http:// library.athabascau.ca/ help/guide/guide2research.html

Boyd, D. R. (2001). *Canada vs. the OECD: An environmental comparison.* Retrieved from http:// www.environmentalindicators.com/htdocs/execsum.htm

43 Article from a Web Site (No Date)

Haas, S. (n.d.). Acoustical considerations: An introduction. *Dezignare.* Retrieved from http://www.dezignare.com/ newsletter/acoustics.html

44 Article from a Web Site (No Author, No Date)

Canadian Environmental Network. (n.d.). *Tools and links: Environmental petitions process.* Retrieved from http://www.cen-rce.org/eng/links.html

When no author is available, find the name of the home page and cite as the author.

45 Article from a Database (With DOI)

Buske-Kirschbaum, A., Ebrecht, M., Kern, S., Gierens, A.,
    & Hellhammer, D. H. (2008). Personality characteristics
    in chronic and non-chronic allergic conditions. *Brain,*
    Behavior & Immunity, 22(5), 762-768. doi:10.1016/
    j.bbi.2007.12.002

46 Article from a Database (No DOI)

Lertzman, D.A., & Vredenburg, H. (2005, February). Indigenous
    peoples, resource extraction and sustainable development: An
    ethical approach. *Journal of Business Ethics, 56*(3), 239-254.
    Retrieved from http://www.philinfo.org.

**If a journal article has no DOI and is retrieved from
a library database, complete a Web search to find
the home page URL of the journal.**

47 Article in an Internet-only Magazine or Journal (With DOI)

Van Eijck, M., & Roth, W. M. (2007). Improving science
    education for sustainable development. *PLoS Biology,*
    5(12). doi:10.1371/journal.pbio.0050306

48 Article in an Internet-only Magazine or Journal (No Author, No DOI)

The world flips. (2008, May). *Ecologist, 38*(4), 10. Retrieved
    from http://www.theecologist.org

49 Document Available on College/University Program or Department Web Site (No Author, No Date)

Athabasca University. (n.d.). *The AU library guide to the*
    research process. Retrieved from http://library.
    athabascau.ca/help/guide/guide2research.html

50   Encyclopedia or Dictionary (With Editor)

Story, G. M., Kirwin, W. J., & Widdowson, J. D. (Eds.). (1999). *Dictionary of Newfoundland English* (2nd ed.). Retrieved from http://www.heritage.nf.ca/dictionary

51   Entry from an Encyclopedia or Dictionary

Marsh, J. (2008). Inukshuk. In *The Canadian encyclopedia: Historica Foundation of Canada.* Retrieved from http://www. thecanadianencyclopedia.com

52   Entry from an Encyclopedia or Dictionary (No Author)

Hegemony. (n.d.). In *Merriam-Webster's online dictionary.* Retrieved from http://www.merriam-webster.com/ dictionary/hegemony

Where there is no author given, use the word entry in its place.

53   Television/Film/Visual Podcast

CBC Digital Archives. (2008). *Leni Riefenstahl in her own words* [Television interview]. Retrieved from CBC: http://archives.cbc.ca/great_interviews/13940/

Use the director or producer of a film as the author. In square brackets, identify the type of production: Motion picture, Documentary, or Interview.

54   Audio Podcast

Green, C. D. (Producer). (2007). Harry Heft on James J. Gibson, the founder of ecological psychology. *This week in the history of psychology* [Audio podcast]. Retrieved from http://www.yorku.ca/christo/podcasts/ TWITHOP-Jan21.mp3

55 Government Document

> Industry Canada. (2007). *Industry Canada 2007
> General Population Survey Final Report.* Retrieved
> from http://www.ic.gc.ca/epic/site/ic1.nsf/vwapj/
> ICGeneralPopulationSurvey2007-FinalReport.pdf/$file/
> ICGeneralPopulationSurvey2007-FinalReport.pdf

56 Government Document from CD-ROM Database

> Statistics Canada. (1998). *Profile series* (Catalogue no.
> 95F0268XCB960000) [CD-ROM]. Ottawa, ON: Author.

**When the author is a group or corporation, the
publisher is often the same organization. In this
case, give the publisher's name as "Author."**

57 Media Release

> The Office of Aileen Carroll, MPP Barrie. (2008, June
> 20). *Millions in new and innovative community
> programming part of historic Aging at Home
> strategy* [Media release]. Retrieved from http://www.
> aileencarroll.onmpp.ca/pressreleases.aspx?id=18

58 Newspaper Article

> Dube, R. (2008, July 21). Geeks gone wild: Disgruntled IT
> staff wreak havoc. *The Globe and Mail.* Retrieved from
> http://www.theglobeandmail.com

59 Newspaper Article (No Author)

> GE planning fires the "ecoimagination." (2008, March 6).
> *The Toronto Star.* Retrieved from http://www.thestar.com

60 Online Brochure

Community Legal Education Ontario. (2007). *Do you know a woman who is being abused?* [Brochure]. Retrieved from http://www.cleo.on.ca/english/abuse/abused.pdf

61 Online Book

Thoreau, H. D. (2004, June 12). *On the duty of civil disobedience.* Retrieved from http:// www.gutenberg.org/ files/71/71-h/71-h.htm (Original work published 1849)

62 Online Book with Corporate Author

Public Health Agency of Canada. (2006). *Canadian immunization guide: 2006* (7th ed.). Retrieved from http://www.phac-aspc.gc.ca/publicat/cig-gci/pdf/cig-gci-2006_e.pdf

63 Online Message Postings

Online message postings include blogs, news or discussion groups, forums, and mailing lists.

Galloway, G. (2009, October 14). What this woman wants. [Web log post]. Retrieved from http://www.theglobeandmail.com/blogs/witness-kandahar/what-this-woman-wants/article1323478/

Papillion. (2009, October 15). Re: What this woman wants. [Web log comment]. Retrieved from http://www.theglobeandmail.com/blogs/witness-kandahar/what-this-woman-wants/article1323478/

Use the author's name, if available, or screen name.

Do not use italics for the title, subject, or thread.

Identify the type of posting in square brackets following the titles, e.g., [Web log post].

In the retrieval statement, give the URL where the message can be retrieved.

64 Wiki

Terror management theory (TMT). (2008, April 29).
   Retrieved July 25, 2008, from Psychwiki: http://
   www.psychwiki.com/wiki/Terror_Management_
   Theory_%28TMT%29

Wikis are Web pages with ever-changing content where public users contribute to and edit the articles. Since the authorship is collaborative, and therefore unknown, insert the title of the article as author. Include the retrieval date and name of the Wiki in the retrieval statement.

65 Thesis Retrieved from a Database

Teixeira, H. M. (2003). *The sovereignty of governed*
   populations: An inquiry into the displacement of the
   common good in modern political thought (Doctoral
   dissertation). Available from ProQuest Digital
   Dissertations. (AAT NQ88728)

Include the database name in the retrieval statement followed by the accession or order number if one is assigned.

66   **Review of a Book/Film/Performance**

Thomas, C. (2008, January/February). Unearthing a part
of the underground railroad [Review of the book *I've got
a home in glory land: A lost tale of the underground
railroad,* by K. Smardz-Frost]. *Books in Canada, 37*(1),
13-14. Retrieved from http://www.booksincanada.com

Use the reviewer's name as the author.

67   **Curriculum Guide**

Manitoba Education, Citizenship and Youth. (2007).
*Kindergarten to grade 12 Aboriginal languages and
cultures: Manitoba curriculum framework of outcomes.*
Retrieved from http://www.edu.gov.mb.ca/k12/abedu/
framework/k-12_ab_lang.pdf

68   **Video blog post**

Carroll, D. (2009, July 7). United breaks guitars [Video
file]. Retrieved from http://www.youtube.com/
watch?v=5YGc4zOqozo&feature=fvw

Index

Index

Index

Index

Index

Index

ACKNOWLEDGEMENT FOR QUOTATIONS ACCOMPANYING PHOTOGRAPHS

Bates, H. W. (2005). *The naturalist on the river Amazons.* Boston: Adamant Media. (Original work published 1873)

Flannery, T. (2005) *The weather makers.* Toronto: HarperCollins.

Jensen, J. (1990). *Siftings.* Baltimore: Johns Hopkins University Press. (Original work published 1939)

Leopold, A. (2001). *A Sand County almanac.* New York: Oxford University Press. (Original work published 1949)

Olson, S. F. (1958). *Listening point.* New York: Alfred A. Knopf.

Thoreau, H. D. (1866). Civil Disobedience. In *A yankee in Canada, with anti-slavery and reform papers* (pp. 123-151). Boston: Ticknor and Fields.

ADDITIONAL INFORMATION

For additional information, consult the following manual, available in libraries:

American Psychological Association. (2010). *Publication manual of the American Psychological Association.* (6th ed.). Washington, DC: American Psychological Association.

APA Web Site

You can also visit the APA Web site, which provides format suggestions and examples at **http://www.apastyle.org**